the **Canary**

A guide to selection, housing, care,

nutrition, behaviour, health, breeding

and mutations

Contents

Foreword

Canaries have been kept as pets for centuries, both for their attractive plumage colours as well as their melodious songs. Many pet canary owners have developed their hobby further, by breeding and ultimately exhibiting their birds, at local, national and international exhibitions, held in many countries, throughout the world.

As long as a bird's well-being is taken seriously, keeping and caring for a canary can be a very satisfying hobby. As with any animal though, when you take on a canary you taken on the obligations that come with it. The bird's well-being will be entirely in your hands and it will only thrive if you have a reasonable understanding of it's housing needs, nutritional needs and it's behaviour.

This small book covers many aspects of keeping and caring for canaries, including information about several varieties that exist and it will provide you as a budding bird enthusiast with most of the basic information you need to keep your own canary responsibly.

Having kept canaries for more than forty years as a successful breeder, champion exhibitor and international judge, I am delighted to recommend this book to all those considering taking up the hobby. The knowledge it contains will ensure you are well equipped to look after your new charges, and will act as a useful reference point, for many years to come.

My own specialist interest lies with the Yorkshire canary, developed in the UK over 150 years ago, as a a Type or Posture canary, a specialist exhibition bird known colloquially as "the Gentleman of the Fancy" due to its upright position and bold, fearless attitude. To gain a better insight into Yorkshire canaries, please visit my website www.geocities.com/briaankeenanuk.

We hope you enjoy reading this book, as you set out in the hobby of canary keeping.

Brian Keenan
Merseyside
England
July 2003

about pets

A Publication of About Pets.

Copyright © 2003
About Pets
co-publisher United Kingdom
Kingdom Books
PO9 5TL, England

ISBN 1852792027
First printing
September 2003

Original title: *de Kanarie*
© 2002 Welzo Media Productions bv,
About Pets bv,
Warffum, the Netherlands
http://www.aboutpets.info

Photos:
Rob Doolaard,
Ton Ebben,
Tini Houtzager,
Rob Dekker,
Dirk Van den Abeele,
Theo Beerenfanger
Europet
and Pieter van den Hooven

Printed in Italy

In general

The Spanish imported the canary from it's Canary Islands home from the 15e century onwards for its tuneful song and it's been considered a household pet now for centuries primarily for the male's song. The majority of females don't sing a complete song, although many will develop pleasing calls and trills.

How it all started

Canary breeding became profitable and an attempt was made to control the market as the business expanded from Spain by exporting only male birds. Despite the attempt breeding spread to Italy when females were included in a number of shipments by mistake. From Italy it spread further to countries like Austria, Switzerland and Germany although the canary's song was developed mainly in Germany where mineworkers in particular became involved in their breeding. Thousands of song canaries were bred in the village of St.Andreasberg in the German Hartz Mountains for example to be shipped to via Hamburg to America. Dealers carried hundreds of birds to The Netherlands and Belgium by foot. A visit to the Harzer Roller Museum, in the grounds of the former Samson silver mine, and to the mine itself, is really worthwhile for canary fanciers interested in the history and development of song canary breeding.

Canaries, known as Type canaries, were also bred in Spain for markets in France, Belgium, The Netherlands and England where the bird's form, size and structure of the plumage were the main attraction.

As the distribution spread into Europe, larger groups of breeders began to develop the plumage colours. Mutations in the original grey/green colouring that had soon started to appear in captivity were developed, resulting in the appearance of canaries that were virtually yellow. Further developments contributed to the appearance of other popular colours.

Buying

One of most important responsibilities that buying a canary brings with it is for the bird's health. A bird's state of health can often be judged just by looking at it, so it's very important to examine a bird before you hand over any money.

A healthy canary should have clear eyes and be quite lively. Its body, including the lower body, should be covered with snugly fitting healthy looking feathers. If it's sitting puffed up like a ball and trembling on it's perch, or hiding in the corner of the aviary, it's not going to be a good buy.

If you're looking for a song canary for company it's important to buy one from a reputable pet shop. Most shops stock canaries obtained from known breeders but there is no reason why you shouldn't buy direct from a breeder yourself. If you buy from a breeder, you should also be able to learn something about your bird's parents.

Canaries for aviaries

If you are buying canaries for a communal aviary you'll need to ensure that there are more females than males in the group or limit yourself to keeping one or two, in which case you'll have to accept the fact that the male will hardly sing at all. Blood will be shed if two males are placed in a cage together although this behaviour is less likely to occur where a distinct hierarchy develops where each bird is able to claim and defend it's own perch.

Leg bands

When buying your canary check to see if the bird has been banded. If it has, the band will show the bird's date of birth which is handy to know if you're buying a male for his singing ability because males will only sing well when they are at least ten months old, mature and have had their first moult.

The bird will need a little time to get used to the new surroundings. It can take up to fourteen days or so before a new bird will start singing, but if it hasn't started after this time it's best to take it back to the pet shop or to the breeder you bought it from to have them confirm that it's definitely a male. Experienced canary fanciers and breeders will know what to look for. A healthy male placed in a suitable cage will show that it's at ease by singing. If the canary is going to be kept in a cage in your living room it's important to remember that it also needs sleep and make sure that it's not exposed to light for more than fifteen hours in any one day. The cage should be covered at night to make sleep possible. Aviary canaries adjust to natural light hours themselves.

Housing

Canaries have become domesticated over a long period of time to become cage or aviary birds that can rarely survive now in the wild, so you'll need to provide them with a secure home of which various types are available.

Vertical bars

The first aspect to consider when choosing a bird's home is health. The wrong type of accommodation can lead to irreversible damage to a bird's health and make it vulnerable to sicknesses. An equally important consideration is the amount of space available. If the canary is going to be kept as a solitary pet a good quality cage can be bought at a pet shop. When you're buying the cage pay a little attention to the bars. The bars should be vertical. Canaries in any case are not fanatical climbers. The cage needs to be easy to clean thoroughly without too much risk of the bird escaping.

Bird fanciers who keep canaries often help to maintain the population by continuing the breeding process but Canaries need space and the number you'll be able to keep yourself will depend upon the amount of space available to you. A spacious birdhouse linked to a flight cage is the ideal solution but not everybody has this sort of space available and most canary fanciers have to be content with something more conservative such as a shed, a spare room or an attic. As long as a few sensible basic conditions are met, it's an enjoyable hobby.

Instructions on how to build a birdhouse are beyond the scope of this small book so if you need advice and assistance it's best to ask an experienced canary keeper.

Flying space

The birds will need a flight cage or flying space if they're to learn and develop their flying skills. If you keep your canary in a cage you can try opening the cage door after it's had time to get acclimatised to it's surroundings and let it find it's own way out. As long as you keep an eye on things, the bird can explore the room, sit on your shoulder and maybe even eat at the table with you, but the moment a door or window are left open your canary will be gone.

Fitting out a cage or aviary
Aviary birds generally have enough flying space but you'll need to ensure that there are sufficient perches available for each bird to be able claim it's own. Anybody observing a group of canaries closely will notice in time that a hierarchy exists in which each bird must have it's own place.

The birds will spend a comparatively long time in an aviary, so it must be practical and easy to clean. Apart from dust and droppings, poorly sited drinking water holders and birdbaths create the worst pollution. Most of the time this can be avoided simply by positioning perches with some thought. If you can make perches yourself so much the better, but they can be bought ready made. Each ready-made perch is suitable for a single bird and has a roof-like plastic cover that prevents birds from fouling each other. Some perches also have a feeding

tray. The perch itself should not be too thin: they are the right size when a canary is not quite able to relax its toes.

Perches should never be placed above feed or water holders. Like bird baths, feed and water holders need to be placed where there will be the least chance of the contents becoming contaminated: it's best to fix them inside the front of the cage so that they hang over or sit in a spill tray to prevent spills from being scattered through the birdhouse. Scattered feed can be contaminated very easily, so it's important to make sure that the birds can't eat it. The same applies to contaminated drinking water. The cage or aviary litter is also very important but you can read about this topic later in the booklet.

Dimensions
The size of the flying area depends mainly on the size of the accommodation. For the bird's well-being it's important to limit the number you keep to the capacity of the available space. An area that's too small or has too many birds in it will provoke aggressive behaviour and produce irreversible unrest within the group and lead to the birds picking at each other's feathers.

Climate
Aside from keeping the Canary's accommodation clean, the climate needs to be comfortable. For the most part you can control this yourself so it's important to know a little about ventilation, heating, air, humidity and lighting.

Ventilation
The air in the cage needs to be refreshed constantly with clean air without draughts being created that could result in sicknesses developing. Ventilation can be provided mechanically with an electric fan or naturally using air vents. The vents must in any event be mice and insect proof. Fresh air ventilation is important for the climate of the cage and to ensure that dust contaminated air is expelled.

Heating
It's not essential to heat canary cages because well acclimatised birds can survive the winter without it but it's not unusual for cages to be heated either, especially if a breeder wants to start the breeding season earlier than normal. If breeding were to be started in an unheated cage early in the months of January and February when frost could be expected, there would be a risk of the eggs cooling to the degree that production would suffer. Heating, however, is often fitted more for the good of the owner than for the birds.

Should you decide to install heating, you'll need to increase the temperature gradually until it reaches a constant 64° Fahrenheit (18° Celsius) and keep an eye on it from then on to avoid large fluctuations. To be able to maintain the temperature, it's important that the cage be insulated to limit heat loss. You can use one of a number of heat sources but it's vital that any combustion gasses produced are ducted to the outside air and are not allowed to enter the cage.

Air and humidity
The oxygen and humidity levels in the birdhouse need to be balanced. A canary uses a lot of oxygen to convert it's feed into energy because of it's high (105.8° Fahrenheit (41° Celsius)) body temperature but eggs need to "breathe" as well during incuba-

tion and too little oxygen will influence hatching. You can ensure that enough oxygen is always available by using suitable ventilation.

Air humidity is very important and successful egg hatching depends on it being just right. Although the air in a birdhouse will tend to be dry if heating is used, it can just as easily become too humid causing stored food to become damp and unusable.

Birds will be comfortable if you keep the ambient temperature between 64.4 and 68° Fahrenheit, (18 and 20° Celsius) and the air humidity between 60 and 70%. You can check the degree of humidity with a hygrometer and adjust it your-

self as follows:
- with an electrical air humidifier
- by placing dishes of water on a heat source
- by ensuring a good supply of oxygen through ventilation
- by providing the birds with bath-water
- by spraying the birds and the eggs with water from a plant spray

Always use fresh, tepid water when you are spraying birds and eggs because water that's been sitting around in a plant spray for a few days will have already become contaminated enough to cause serious bacterial infection if used.

Canaries produce lots of dust and the air will inevitably become dusty, but lightly contaminated air can be easily purified with an ioniser. Ionisation is the process of producing the right ratio of positive ions and negative ions. An ioniser refreshes contaminated air deficient in positive ions by producing air that's rich in negative ions. The result experienced is 'mountain air', which will make everybody feel good, including the birds.

A multiple action air cleaner is also useful for purifying air. Dust particles are trapped electro-statically, a carbon filter removes stale air and what remains is refreshed and cleaned of microscopic particles and the ion balance improved by ionisation.

Lighting
Canaries need sunlight, especially the UV radiation required to produce the essential vitamin D3, for them to remain at their best. The construction of a birdhouse should allow as much natural sunlight to enter it as possible. Artificial light can be used to supplement natural light as necessary, although there are occasions where natural light might be replaced entirely by artificial light.

It's best to use a fluorescent light fitted with two full spectrum 'natural day light' fluorescent tubes
and an electronic starter as the main lighting because, unlike older models, these fittings produ-

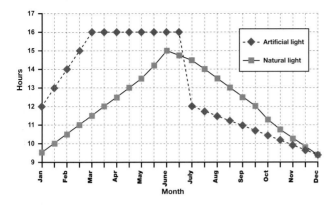

ce flicker-free light. Even though flickering in the older types is barely perceptible to the human eye, canaries see these lamps switching on and off 50 times per second. In addition to fluorescent tubes, you can use regular low-wattage low-intensity lamps to simulate sunrise and sunset by switching them on before turning the main lighting on or off. Both sorts of lighting can be controlled using a time switch.

An up-to-date way of controlling lighting is to use an electronic dimmer combined with a high frequency fluorescent tube fitting. This way, light output can be regulated automatically and a single unit will provide light and simulate dawn and dusk. The flicker-free light will also be better for the bird's health. Various makes of electronic controllers are available in the shops.

Increasing the lighting time
During the resting season, with it's long nights, Canaries don't need any more light than the 12 hours of daylight provided naturally. If you want to start the breeding season earlier than the traditional March 19th, however, you'll need to increase the birds' lighting hours over a period of seven weeks to about 15 or 16 hours a day. This includes dawn and dusk. You can use a clock timer adjusting it with care to gradually increase the lighting hours. Once the full lighting time has been reached, you won't need to make any further changes to the settings. Don't change the time settings even when local time changes from wintertime to summertime. The birds will adapt to the programmed time but fluctuations should be avoided so as not to disturb their biorhythm.

You can use the following table if you want to increase the lighting time. It assumes a regular lighting time of 12 hours per day.

Care

Apart from housing, there are other aspects of care that need to be taken into account once you've made that decision to keep canaries.

Bathing

Canaries love to take baths and look after their feathers, so it's important to give them the opportunity. You can attach a bathhouse to the inside front of the cage or aviary or you can put a dish of water on the floor, but if you use a dish you'll need to make sure that it stands on a support and not directly on the floor. Healthy birds will start to use the bath soon after it's been put in place and the water will become dirty quite quickly with bird droppings and dust from the feathers. To prevent the birds drinking contaminated water, the bath needs to be made available to a fixed schedule and never allowed to stand for more than a couple of hours at a time.

Litter

It's important to use a good quality litter to prevent the canaries' plumage getting damaged. The covering has to be able to absorb moisture, for example from bird droppings, drinking water and bath water spills, because damp spots are a breeding ground for infections. It also needs to be dust free and safe for birds. A bird might digest a fine type of covering without it actually harming the bird's digestive system. Another litter type might pass through the bird without any problem at all but others, such as silver sand, will block the bird's intestines. The best covering to use is the most environmentally friendly and biologically degradable material you can find.

There are many sorts of covering now available so choose the one that you want. These days, natural products such as beech wood chippings, hemp fibre, recycled paper pulp or a product made from the hard core of the corncob often replaces the traditional silver sand. Barred cages are being produced in some countries that use a floor lining made of carton. The carton is mounted on a roll at the side of the cage. When the lining becomes soiled a new piece can be pulled off the roll and through the cage. Should you decide to use a litter that has no gravel or grit in it, bear in mind that you'll need to provide this separately for your canaries. If you're not sure which litter is best for your cage or aviary, don't hesitate to ask for advice at your pet shop or from an experienced canary keeper or breeder.

The care routine

Maintaining a high level of hygiene will help prevent a host of problems such as sicknesses, so it's important that a number of care tasks are carried out, some daily others weekly, monthly or even just a few times a year. As a cana-

ry keeper new to the hobby, you'll need to develop your own fixed routine to ensure that you pick up possible changes in your birds condition quickly

Daily care activities
- Remove stale water and feed remains (also remove dirty grit and stomach gravel)
- Clean drink and feed containers (those containing grit and stomach gravel)
- Refill feed and drink containers with fresh feed and drinking water
- Supply fresh bath water
- Remove dirty bath water (after about 2 hours)
- Clean the cage floor

- Check that the seed and drinking containers can still be fixed securely in place
- Check that all doors close well and that no holes can be found anywhere in the cage or aviary.
- Check the birds for possible abnormalities or injuries (this normally happens automatically while you're working with the birds)

Weekly care activities
- Clean the cage or aviary, including the perches and other resting places
- Thoroughly clean feed and drinking trays, removing any deposits
- Replace the litter
- Thoroughly clean the floor
- Rake any natural litter as necessary
- Clean other objects in the aviary such as stones, tiles etc.

Monthly care activities
- Examine the birds for vermin (fleas)
- Check that their nails are the correct length
- Check the cage or aviary for possible holes

Quarterly care activities
- Treat the cage or aviary and all items in it with disinfectant
- Replace natural branches and twigs
- Dig over any natural litter

Feeding

In captivity canaries are completely dependant on their keeper for nutrition. It seems simple enough but there is more to it than simply going to a pet shop, buying the food and giving it to the birds.

Incorrect feeding is the most common reason for unnecessary ailments caused by mistakes that stem from ignorance so it's important to know the variety of canary you have. Is it a song canary, a coloured canary or a Type canary? You'll find all the basic information you need about feeding canaries in this chapter.

Bread and water?
Canaries can survive on a "bread and water" type ration of seed and water, but don't expect too much of them in that case. If you want them to breed successfully, to be able to take part in exhibitions and build up their resistance against illnesses, you'll need to get acquainted with their feeding requirements.

The intensive contacts that feed suppliers maintain with bird fanciers means that they are well aware of the special demands that feeding imposes and explains why they're able to offer highly suitable feeds. To be able to make the right choice from what's on offer it's important to know a little about bird feed and specifically the needs of the different groups of canaries.

The value of feed
Birds need nutrition to:
• be able to develop into adult animals
• stay alive and be able to build up resistance to sicknesses
• get into good breeding condition

Each of the above imposes specific nutritional requirements. Birds use

nutrition to produce energy and the energy in turn is used to produce body heat and power activities such as breathing, walking, flying, forming protein, building muscle, skin and feathers and producing eggs.

Canaries can only extract the energy they need from their feed if it includes the right ingredients in the first place, so a varied diet is essential to ensure that the correct balance is obtained for conversion into energy. Use of the wrong feed will result in uneven conversion into energy and allow ailments to develop.

Feed factors
The canary is a seedeater. Its beak is well adapted to peeling seeds and the digestion system is designed to convert them into absorbable foodstuffs, although when it's allowed to forage for food the canary will also eat vegetables, fruit and even insects.

Your canary won't be able to obtain all the nutrition it needs from just one sort of seed, so you-'ll need to provide it with a balanced, high quality seed mix. Don't allow the quality to suffer just for the sake of saving money. Seed prices fluctuate on the world market, and that in turn has an effect not only on the retail price but sometimes the quality of the mixes available, especially the cheaper mixes. As far as your bir-

d's health is concerned, always keep in mind that a cheap option can end up being expensive.

The complete canary diet
In addition to a seed mix, the canary needs soft feed to which individual supplements can be added as necessary. To keep a canary in the best possible condition, also for breeding, the diet needs to consist of at least the following ingredients:
• a good mix of seeds
• strength/egg feed, possibly with vitamin supplements
• greens and/or fruit
• supplemental seeds (snacks or treats)
• drinking water
• stomach gravel
• mineral grit

This diet will provide the canary with all the essential elements it needs such as fats, water, carbohydrates, minerals, protein and vitamins. It also needs oxygen of course. This sounds obvious but cage air is often contaminated with dust and bacteria.

Feed quality
Whilst a balanced diet will provide your birds with all the nutrition they need, even high quality manufactured feeds will suffer if they're not handled and stored properly. Feed should not be exposed to sunlight, high temperatures, air, or to damp surroundings. Due to the fat content, feed will beco-

me rancid within a couple of weeks if it's kept under poor conditions and if it's then given to the birds it will result in a severe vitamin E deficiency. Buying too much feed at a time will also lead to a lowering in the quality simply because it will take too long to use up the supply.

Special equipment can be used to make undigested but used seed reusable but it's not recommended. The seeds are infected with bacteria, moulds and germs and even after processing they will not have been readjusted to provide the correct nutritional value. The importance of buying a good quality balanced seed mix for your canaries can't be overstated. It may not be cheap but in the long run it will pay for itself. Try to make as little mess as possible and use a rationing system for feeding your birds.

Although a wide variety of good mixes are available, you can also have a mix made up at a pet shop to your own requirements, however a little know-how is needed to avoid making potentially serious mistakes. You would do well to

Egg food ingredients

ask an experienced breeder for advice before putting your own mix together.

Soft feed

Even the best seed mixes don't include all the nutrition needed so soft feed has to be provided as well, especially to young birds until they're able to peel seeds for themselves. Soft feed can be divided up into egg, stamina and breeding feed.

Egg feed

Egg feed is a soft feed that's prepared with egg or egg products that are high in protein as the name indicates. The very best egg feed is a mixture of bread and very fresh high quality eggs, such as free range eggs. You can make the mix yourself possibly adding some feed supplements. A good homemade egg feed is a hardboiled egg (boil for 7 minutes) mixed with three crushed rusks and an appropriate amount of supplements. It must always be freshly made. Some ready-to-use egg feeds are available too, although the amount of protein contained in each differs so you will need to check the lysine and methionine content from the package at the time of purchase. The higher the percentage, the better the feed will be for the birds.

Egg food

Apart from the seasons when canaries are breeding and feeding their young they also need protein during the resting and moulting seasons, so don't limit egg feed just to the breeding season. The advantage of feeding birds suitable doses throughout the year is that they will already be acclimatised to the feed at the start of each new breeding season when they need it most.

Stamina and breeding feed

Stamina and breeding feed is a maintenance and conditioning seed mix supplement that needs to be given primarily during the rest and moulting seasons. This feed contains all essential amino acids, vegetable proteins, vitamins and minerals, and needs to be as fresh as possible. Once a pack has been opened it must be kept in a sealed container to prevent it from getting damp or becoming contaminated by dust. The pack often displays a production date or a "use by" date.

Changing to other feed

One day sooner or later you might decide to change from one soft feed to another because the one you are using isn't living up to your expectations. You can avoid the new feed being rejected by making the changeover a gradual one. Start by mixing a little of the new feed with your existing feed so that the birds gradually get used to it.

Green feed

It's' easy to see from the damage often done to aviary plants and bushes that canaries love to eat green feed. Green feed is an excellent supplement, but you need to take care when using it to

The function of vitamins in birds

Vitamin A	Mainly available for recessive white canaries, use in combination with vitamin E
Vitamin E	Better known as wheat germ oil, is also available as a powder
Vitamin K	Apart from being a blood coagulator also good against the birds plucking each other
Vitamin A and D	For the production of bone and egg shell
Vitamin A and D3	Found in cod-liver oil
Vitamin B	When using antibiotics
Vitamin H	Is Vitamin B7 or Biotin, for producing a good feather structure and growth

avoid over-feeding, which can be damaging, especially with green feed because it consists mainly of water and too much water in green feed can result in diarrhoea.

Another danger lurks in the way vegetables are cultivated. Preventive spraying with insecticides and fungicides means that traces of these agents may still be present on vegetables. Take care also when feeding with weeds. Canaries love chickweed but if it's been gathered in the wild it may be strongly contaminated with animal droppings and the possibility of infection and sickness could be considerable.

Green feed must always be thoroughly washed and dried before it's given to canaries. Bear in mind that a number of vegetables contain high concentrations of carotene that can lead to impurities appearing in feather colours.

Health seeds or treats

Health seeds will add variety to a canary's regular seed mix, but it's additional feed so it needs to be given sparingly. Weed seeds are very popular too but if you gather them yourself it will be difficult to tell whether they are contaminated with pesticides or fungicides. Like some vegetables, they also can have a negative effect on the purity of feather colours so all things considered it's best to use commercially produced mixes sold at pet shops as Health Seeds.

Supplements

Supplements are added to the diet for two reasons:
- to complete or provide variation in regular food
- to compensate for possible feed deficiencies and to correct feeding errors

(Multi)vitamins

Canaries will normally obtain all the vitamins they need from a balanced diet but it still might become necessary to add individual vitamins to their feed, for example if feeding has gone wrong. It's better to use products available at pet shops rather than to experiment yourself with individual vitamins.

A multi-vitamin is a preventative supplement made up of 12 types of vitamins that can be given to stimulate moulting, maintain physical condition and healthy, shiny feathers. Multi-vitamins can compensate for deficiencies and they are soluble so they can be given dissolved in drinking water. For the correct dosage either consult the instructions on the pack or follow your vet's instructions.

Cuttlebone

Herbs

A little time spent observing birds in the wild will show that that they eat herbs in addition to seeds. Apart from their nutritional value, herbs are also known to have healing properties so adding them together with vitamins, trace ele-

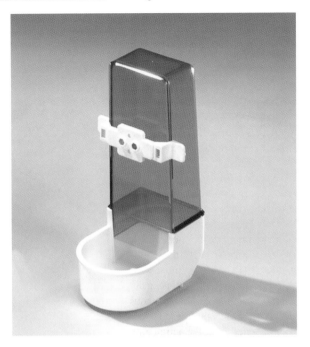

made from extracts of the purest Norwegian seaweed, aids the production of pigments and stimulates the metabolism.

Drinking water

All living creatures, including canaries, need water. Water serves as a temperature regulator, an internal dilutant and transport for nutrients. Canaries need fresh, clean drinking water and it can't be emphasised enough that it really does need to be fresh and clean. All too often drinking dish and fountain water contaminated by feed remains, droppings and sun stimulated algae growth isn't replaced until the last drop has been used up.

What would normally be an essential source of health becomes a breeding place for a host of sicknesses. Any contamination or water additive can become a breeding ground for sicknesses, so simply adding a germicide isn't enough. Problems can easily be prevented by changing the water on a daily basis and by cleaning the water dish or drinking fountain thoroughly several times a week.

One way to prevent drinking water from becoming contaminated is to use an inverted water bottle and tube. The tube is made of stainless steel and the open end projecting from the bottle is closed with a metal ball lightly

ments and minerals to bird feed can help a bird's organs to function properly. Bird herbs were introduced onto the market no so long ago for use with canaries, but buy them in moderation because, while it's true that birds eat herbs, they don't eat them in large quantities.

Sea algae

Sea algae contain large amounts of naturally pure minerals, trace elements and variety of vitamins so they're a perfect supplement to a pet's daily feed, certainly for canaries. Sea algae can aid recovery and prevent sicknesses caused by incorrect feeding. It's also known that the product, which is enough to ensure that a drop of water always forms to hang under the tube. It's important to make sure that that drinking water is always available so the water should always be boiled before use to ensure that the steel ball doesn't become stuck with lime scale deposits, especially if the drinking tube is not going to be checked regularly.

Stomach gravel

All the nutrients needed by a bird for it to stay in top physical condition should come from its feed, which the digestion process breaks down into a solution easily absorbed by the blood. A bird's digestive system is a complex arrangement of organs that process feed both mechanically and chemically. Birds have no teeth so they have a muscled stomach that grinds feed mechanically and they swallow gravel to help the process.

For the grinding process to work best the tiny stones the birds swallow have to be sharp. In the wild the birds find these stones themselves, so this of course presents a problem for birds in captivity. In recent years a number of new products have come onto the market promoted as the ideal solution for birdcage litter but the modern coverings don't contain the small stones birds need to help digestion. Traditional litters such as river sand contain an enormous amount of stones but these have been rounded by wave action and have little or no grinding effect.

If you are going to use modern litters, the best solution is to buy gravel that you'll find labelled mostly as 'sharp stomach gravel'. Older publications don't mention gravel but they do mention grit and sepia although neither of these have a grinding effect in the stomach. Sharp stomach gravel is manufactured by crushing pebbles and it's available in a variety of sizes for various birds. Sharp stomach gravel not only makes certain that feed is thoroughly ground up, it also ensures that it's used more efficiently, which in turn means that birds will stay in shape with less. Over time, gravel is expelled from the stomach as it becomes worn and rounded so it's important that a bird always has access to a supply of the correct type of sharp stomach gravel in the birdhouse. Sharp stomach gravel is also added to factory-mixed bird grit, but grit is not the same as gravel.

Mineral grit

Canaries will obtain the minerals they need including calcium, as long as they are fed a combination of a good seed mix and soft feed, to which a quantity of calcium has been added. The need for calcium, however, is variable and birds can absorb too much if you are also adding products containing calcium to manufactured soft feed or homemade soft feed. To prevent over-dosage, always provide them with separate grit throughout the year so that they can decide for themselves when and how much calcium they consume.

Grit is a simple product consisting of ground, roasted oyster shells. It's available in various sizes especially for canaries. Grit can be bought at pet shops in different forms, but the sort that's easiest to check is the loose variety that contains no abnormal additives. Factory packed grit is also available, but it often contains additives that the bird fancier would prefer not to have included such as limestone, red stone and charcoal. Calcium rich seaweed and stomach gravel are useful canary supplements.

Bird minerals

The need for calcium is greatest in the breeding season and bird minerals have been brought onto the market to satisfy this demand. The percentages of calcium, phosphorous and sodium in these products are higher than those found in normal grit but, like grit, they should be made available to the birds separately and not mixed with soft food. Grit has no milling or grinding qualities and is digested in the canary's stomach without adding anything itself to the digestion process, which is why stomach gravel is necessary.

Health and sickness

The basic principle of keeping canaries is to keep them healthy. Despite this situations do arise unexpectedly with one or more birds suddenly in a poor condition or showing signs of sickness.

It's often difficult to diagnose which sickness you are dealing with because canaries can be exposed to any number of sicknesses ranging from mild to serious. The most important and common ailments can be found in this chapter, together with tips on diagnosis and treatment.

Understanding the sicknesses that affect birds is a specialisation even within the world of animal medicine so it's not a good idea as a bird fancier to experiment when a number of birds suddenly get sick or die. If you're ever confronted with large-scale problems it's best to consult a bird specialist vet and let him or her make the diagnosis and prescribe the correct treatment. Without a little advice and medicine from a vet you'll be able to handle things yourself only in a small number of cases.

Sources of infection

Sicknesses can develop in birds with resistance reduced by vitamin deficiency when they come into contact with one of a number of infections, and this infection is then able to slip through their natural defences. Sicknesses such as: parasites, bacteria, viruses, fungus infections and protozoa.

It's not unthinkable that you might have made a mistake yourself involving housing, feeding or care and are then confronted with sickness and abnormalities caused by:
• parasites such as mites, lice and worms
• accidents (trauma)
• abnormalities with moulting

- blockages
- obesity
- egg-binding

The main sickness groups

Canary sicknesses can be divided into two main groups, non infectious and infectious.

Infection

Your birds can become infected in a number of ways. Newly bought birds might have already been sick, flying and stinging insects can transfer sicknesses but above all rodents, wild birds, rainwater and even you could be responsible.

New birds

To avoid the healthy birds you may already have being infected by newcomers, you need to take precautions when acquiring new birds and it's important to check a new bird's origin. If you're buying at a bird market, a pet shop of through a third party it's often difficult to obtain any information so it's wise to obtain birds direct from a breeder.

Quarantine

If new birds are obtained without satisfactory background information on them being available, you can best isolate them from the other birds by placing them in quarantine. It's difficult to be precise about how long the quarantine period should be because it can differ by variety, but the minimum should be six weeks. Even then, symptoms don't always appear, but it will at least give you the opportunity to keep them under observation and check for any signs of infection while they acclimatise themselves to their accommodation, feed, lighting and heating conditions.

Birds can also be carriers and spread infections over a long period of time without ever developing symptoms themselves.

Flying and stinging insects

Mosquitoes and flies can spread diseases by attacking mainly sleeping birds, sucking their blood and causing inflammation and infection in their feet and toes. Flies present an additional danger

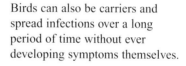

Non infectious sicknesses	Infectious sicknesses
gastro-enteritis	atoxoplasmosis
pneumonia	coccidiosis
kidney abnormalities	canary pox
liver abnormalities	pseudo-tuberculosis
anaemia	paratyphoid (salmonella)
	worm infection
	air sac or trachea mite infection

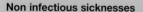

when they're at the larva stage. The grubs live on contaminated material and they're often toxic and dangerous to birds, so it's important to at least try to prevent them from entering the birdhouse even though in most cases it's practically impossible.

Rodents, wild birds, yourself and rain water

Keeping rodents as a hobby doesn't generally combine well with bird keeping because of the importance of keeping rodents out of the birdhouse. Apart from the unrest it creates, rodent droppings and urine are sources of serious infection. The same applies to the droppings of any wild birds that might get into an aviary.

As well as those introduced by rodents and wild birds, infections can be carried in on the clothes and shoes worn by anybody entering the birdhouse. Infections from other birdhouses and even rubbish in the street can infect an otherwise healthy bird population without the origin becoming apparent. It's also possible that unprotected rainwater given to the birds may have been contaminated with wild birds' droppings.

How infections spread

In addition to the possibility of infection from outside the birdhouse, infections coming from inside the birdhouse are just as likely. A number of causes are:
• direct contact between healthy

and sick birds
• sources of infection in feed and drinking water
• sources of infection in bird droppings
• infection via blood-sucking insects
• sources of infection present in the air
• sources of infection on the keeper
• sources of infection on tools or equipment used in the birdhouse

As you can see from this summary, many infections are preventable if errors in care, feeding and housing could be avoided. It's often assumed that simply keeping things clean will prevent infections, but cleanliness alone is not always enough.

Bird hygiene

Healthy canaries instinctively keep themselves clean and spend a lot of time looking after their feathers. Dirty feathers reduce their insulation properties and become an ideal hiding place for all sorts of parasites. Canaries can also keep their feathers clean by taking a bath, even a bath in dry dusty earth helps to remove foreign objects from their feathers.

The preening gland

Apart from being cleaned, feathers also need to be treated to improve and maintain their condition. Many types of birds have a preening gland that secretes an oil-like substance. The beak is rubbed over the preening gland and then over the feathers, especially the flight feathers, coating them with the oil. When exposed to ultraviolet light the oil also has the property of producing vitamin D, which the bird absorbs through its skin while it's cleaning and maintaining its feathers.

It's very important that the surroundings of small birds are kept as clean as possible so as not to attract the attention of large birds of prey. This can cause problems during the time that young birds are developing and dirtying the nest. Songbirds are especially adept at keeping their nest clean and the young birds produce droppings coated in a jelly like packages that are easily disposed of by the parents.

Captive canaries have limited flying space and live in surroundings where debris constantly accumulates. It's the keeper's responsibility to remove the debris regularly to prevent infections from developing.

Symptoms of disease

The majority of canaries will have been sick already for a while by the time it's discovered, so it's important to be able to recognise

Type canary

Coloured show
canaries

the symptoms in time. Below is a list of generally recognisable symptoms.

Posture
- Sick canaries will often sit shaped like a ball with their head buried in their feathers
- Their wings droop
- They sit on the ground in a corner of the birdhouse

Behaviour
- A sick canary may be lethargic but can also display irritated or aggressive behaviour

Appearance
- The feathers no longer fit tightly
- Temperature loss is limited by puffing up the feathers, thickening the insulating air layer around the body
- The eyes are no longer clear or they have become dirty as mucus has dried
- The eyes are often closed or partly closed

Breathing
- The bird has difficulty getting its breath, its body trembles or shakes, often accompanied by rapid breathing

- The canary sneezes or sniffs
- The canary is troubled by voice changes, producing a piping noise for example

Appetite
- The bird looses weight rapidly
- The condition is obvious from inspecting the breastbone muscles

Defecation
- Normal faeces are solid and consist of urea crystals encapsulated in clear white fluid.
- Yellow or green colouring of the faeces indicates liver problems.
- Thin faeces can indicate kidney or intestinal problems.
- Blood in the faeces comes from the last section of the intestines or the urethra.
- Black coloured faeces indicate a haemorrhage in the upper intestine.
- Dirty feathers around the cloaca may indicate diarrhoea.

Canary ailments
Canaries can suffer from a range of bird related sicknesses and other complaints. This paragraph contains a limited summary of canary sicknesses.

Atoxoplasmosis and coccidiosis
Even experts have difficulty in telling these diseases apart. The symptoms in both cases are substantial weight loss, diarrhoea and haemorrhaging in the large intestine. A bird suffering from atoxoplasmosis, depending upon the severity of the infection, may lay its head on the ground as blood vessels in the brain become blocked. Both sicknesses are caused by a parasite that spreads from the intestines to other organs and infection is spread by way of the faeces. Although coccidiosis can be diagnosed by microscopic analysis of the faeces to confirm the presence of the intestinal parasite, this is more difficult with atoxoplasmosis. It's often only possible to confirm the presence of atoxoplasmosis after birds have died from the disease. Good hygiene is the only way to prevent these sicknesses. Medicines that need to be given in doses over a number of days in the drinking water can be obtained from your vet.

Type canary

Canary pox
Canary pox is a virus that's spread amongst other ways by mosquitoes and other stinging insects.

The pox occurs in canaries in three forms:
1. The skin form; external blisters visible on the skin, feet and eyelids
2. The lung form; obvious difficulty with breathing
3. The diphtheria form; internal blisters

Birds infected with pox show clear signs by biting or gasping movements and will suddenly drop dead. The death toll can increase rapidly. You can have

your birds protected against pox by having them vaccinated every year in July or August.

Pseudo-tuberculosis

This sickness may occur in canaries of all ages. The infection can be brought in from outside on shoes, green feeds or by rodents. Although there are no specific symptoms, birds can become seriously ill with lung and intestinal infections. Another characteristic is that a number of birds may suddenly die. Once your vet has made a diagnosis, a course of antibiotics will normally be prescribed, to be given to the birds in their drinking water or feed. Good hygiene is very important.

Worm infection

Birds need to be protected against possible worm infections just like other animals. It's advisable to carry out preventative treatment once a year with roundworm medication. De-worming will reduce the risk of coccidiosis. If you're worming your birds annually, don't use the same medicine every year because worms can become resistant and render the treatment ineffective.

Air sac or tracheal mites

This mite is sometimes found in a bird's windpipe. Hold an infected bird up to a strong light and you may even be able to see them. If your birds are gasping a lot, sneezing, shaking their heads or rubbing their beaks against the perch they may be suffering from tracheal mites.

Infection is by direct contact, which is why quarantining new birds is so important. The birds won't die from the mites but they can become emaciated and their general condition will suffer. Treatment can be given in the form of an inhalation powder or by using IVOMEC, which can be obtained from your vet. Birds not infected will need to be treated if they have been in contact with infected birds.

Red mite

These mites are generally found during the summer and in heated indoor aviaries throughout the year hiding in crevices, cracks and in nesting material, but they doesn't actually live on the birds. They feed mostly at night by crawling over the bird's feet to suck its blood. Signs that red mite may be active are: restlessness, tiredness, pale beaks and feet or difficulty in breathing. Young birds may even die from anaemia. The red mite can be eradicated with a strong insecticide obtained from your vet or agricultural shop.

First aid

You can give a canary first aid the moment you notice its sick while you're waiting for any examination or diagnosis to take place. The two most important initial factors are

warmth and rest so a heated hospital cage where the temperature of the warmest part reaches about 86° Fahrenheit (30° Celsius) is a handy accessory. Birds use less energy to maintain their body weight at about this temperature. Make sure that drinking water and feed bowls are easily accessible to the bird.

When to call the vet

It's common these days for animal owners to have their "own" vet to call on for advice, information and practical help. Every bird fancier should have one simply because it's impossible to predict when their services will be needed and it's important to know in advance who specialises in birds and whom to contact. Vets specialising in birds are widely available these days. In exceptional circumstances, it's even possible to contact vets attached to university clinics. In practice though, most bird owners are inclined to treat sicknesses themselves and although it's sometimes successful if only one bird is involved, if symptoms have already spread to others it's very important that a vet be asked to examine them at an early stage. The bird fancier needs to keep a constant eye on the bird's condition but it's especially important during moulting to avoid overlooking a bird with a 'latent' problem. Canaries that appear to be off colour will often have had a problem for some time and will need to be examined without delay. The bird fancier will rarely be able to do this effectively and may lose time experimenting with various medicines as the bird's condition worsens.

Examination and diagnosis

Examination and diagnosis to identify the cause of a canary's symptoms is best left to a bird specialist vet.

An important examination is to check for infections and parasites and a wide range of tests are available:
- Examination of the faeces. This can be done by microscopic examination or dye test. Amongst other things that will be looked for are internal bacteria, fungus and yeasts.
- Smear tests of the throat, crop, cloaca, skin, etc to help identify parasites. Smear tests may also be used in combination with dye tests and cultures to look for bacterial and fungal infections
- Blood tests to diagnose internal irregularities.

Once a diagnosis has been made your vet will be able to advise you on treatment that will often involve administering medicines obtained either from your vet or from the pet shop. In both cases you should follow the prescribed dosage and never administer a medicine until you have read the accompanying instructions. If you give too much of a medicine the effect can be the opposite of the desired effect.

The canary's annual cycle

The canary's year consists of a number of seasons that the keeper needs to take into account with each requiring special attention. General information on the canary's annual cycle can be found in this chapter. The breeding and the moulting seasons are handled in more detail.

The seasons

The canary's year is divided up as follows:

- Resting season - January to mid-February
- Breeding season - February to June
- Resting season - June to August
- Moulting season - August to September
- Resting season - September to October
- Exhibition season season - October to December

The three most important are: the breeding season, the moulting season and the display season. Your personal motivation for keeping canaries will decide which of the three receives your special attention but if you're keeping a canary for company and its song it's like-

ly to be the moulting season. If you're keeping aviary birds or you're actively breeding colours, all of the seasons will be important to you.

The breeding season

The start of the season is brought on by changes in the length of the day or in the number hours that the birdhouse is lit. By observing your birds regularly the signal that they are ready to begin breeding will be a change in their behaviour. The female will develop a slightly swollen bare lower body with a rearward bulging cloaca. In practice females are ready to breed earlier than males. To start the breeding, the female should be placed alone in the breeding cage with a nest box and some nesting material. If she is ready to breed,

she will start to build a nest immediately. The male should be placed in the cage when the nest is nearly complete. The male will nearly always be accepted as the partner, however when this is not the case it's best to remove him immediately, put him back in the cage on the evening of the same day before the lights go out and remove him again the following morning. This can be repeated as long as necessary until the female has finally accepted the male.

Eggs

About a week after mating the female will lay her first egg followed at intervals normally by another three. Some females start to incubate as soon as the first egg is laid, so to ensure that all the eggs she lays hatch at the same time artificial eggs are sometimes used to replace the laid eggs. However, this is not always necessary, as females already feeding young will feed all their young even if they don't all hatch at the same time.

After the eggs have been incubated for five days or so, it's time to examine them to see if they have all been fertilised. An experienced breeder can often tell at a glance because fertilised eggs appear duller after the incubation period

Just out of the egg

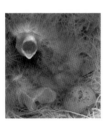

Six days old

than eggs that have not been fertilised. One way to be certain is to shine a strong light through the egg. The content of a fertilised egg will be opaque and clearly visible. If an egg is still transparent after six or seven days it has almost certainly not been fertilised and it's best to remove it from the nest. You can then start the breeding process again.

From egg to bird
Eggs will normally hatch after 13 days during which time the embryo will have developed through a succession of cell divisions into a young bird. In general terms development progresses as follows.

Day 1. The development of the digestive system, creation of the spinal column, nervous system, first blood and the head and eyes begin to form

Day 2. The heart is formed and soon starts to beat

Day 3. Breathing starts and the nose, legs and wings begin to form

Day 4. The tongue and reproductive organs are formed

Day 5. The beak, egg tooth and down begin to develop

Day 6. The beak begins to harden into horn

Day 7. The toenails begin to grow

Day 8. The embryo turns it's head toward the blunt end of the egg

Day 9. The nails and beak become strong and horny

Day 10. The beak turns towards the egg's air chamber

Day 11. The yolk moves alongside the body of the young bird

Day 12. The young bird absorbs the yolk remains

Day 13. The young bird hatches

out having first made a hole in the egg with its egg tooth.

Although the parents don't feed their young for the first 24 hours after hatching, the nutrition in the yolk sack is more than sufficient until the female, and in most cases also the male, start to feed the young birds mainly with soft feed. If the young are well fed, they will need to be ringed after six or seven days but exactly when they can be ringed will depend upon their speed of growth. If they're ringed too early the ring will slide off the foot, if it's attempted too late it won't be possible at all. The young are able to fly after about three weeks during which time the parents continue to feed them, but you can now also give them ground up seed to get them gradually used to seed mix. The young can be separated from their parents about fourteen days after their first flight and placed together with other young birds in a birdhouse.

Although canaries are able to breed three times in a season, it's so exhausting for the female that under normal circumstances it's not wise to allow it. It's better for the female to breed twice in a season.

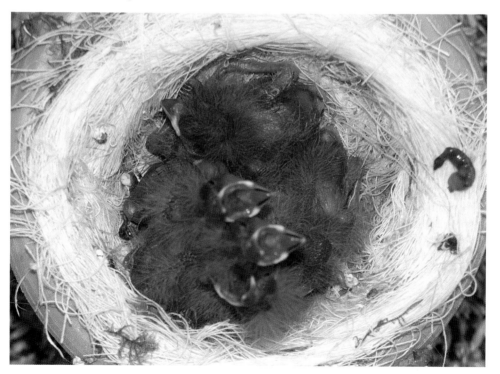

The moulting season

The canary changes its feathers once a year during the moulting season, normally during the months of August and September. Young birds don't moult completely in their first year and their flight, tail and wing feathers only change from the second year.

The canary's colours only become pronounced due to hormonal activity after the first moult. Until then, depending upon the colour, the plumage is generally dull with brown colouring evident in the wing and tail flights and on its back. The fact that wing and tail feathers don't change during the first moult is a disadvantage for the variegated varieties that are not supposed to show any brown in their plumage, but this applies equally to single-colour varieties

where the wings and tails are expected to be colour saturated.

Loss of tail and wing feathers A young canary can lose one or more tail or wing feathers by accident for example during an airborne fight. These feathers take six weeks or so to re-grow but when fully re-grown they will be longer than the original feathers. The difference between regenerated tail feathers and the original feathers can be up to half a centimetre. This means that if a canary loses tail feathers from only one side it will develop an asymmetric tail.

A fully-grown feather actually consists of dead material so it neither grows nor will the metabolic influence of the body change the colour. They can however be effected by external influences.

Think for example of the bleaching effect of the sun on colour pigments. The birds most influenced in this way are the brown and Isabel varieties, especially if these birds are kept in an outdoor aviary constantly exposed to rain and sun. The loss can be so extreme that feathers lack virtually all pigmentation. This comes about due to the effect of ozone principally present in the atmosphere following rain showers and in sunny weather. The original pigmentation returns after moulting.

Moulting normally takes place without any difficulties. The bird sheds and replaces its feathers over a period of days often starting at the breast while the head feathers are the last to change. Nevertheless, it can be a slow process and a canary will be vulnerable during this season if it's in poor condition, unable to bathe regularly or has been exposed to draughts. Medicines are available from pet shops to give stubborn moulting a helping hand but don't hesitate to ask experienced canary keepers for advice.

Red intensive

Canary types and colour varieties

You will have read in the foreword that there are different types of canaries. These are divided into three main groups: song canaries, colour canaries and type canaries.

In this chapter you can read more about these canary varieties, their specific characteristics and mutations.

The difference between canaries is defined both by their individual characteristics and the refinements introduced through the work of breeders. The emphasis in song canaries is on the male's song, in colour canaries on the colour of the feathers and in type or so-called 'posture' canaries on the bird's build and the structure of its plumage. Specialised breeding has produced a range of specific forms and these have divided each of the main groups further into various races, each with their own characteristics.

Song canaries

This is the oldest of the groups for the simple reason that song canaries were the foundation for the development of the sport. The main group of song canaries consists of three breeds: The German (Hartz) Roller, the Waterslager and the Spanish Timbrado.

The German Roller

The German Roller, also known as the Harzer, is a traditional breed specifically developed for its song. Rollers originally came from the Hartz Mountains in Germany and they're easily distinguishable from other song canaries because of the male's complex song tours that are specific to the breed. All the songs have been recorded and are clearly recognisable to true enthusiasts.

The Waterslager

Little has been written about the history of the Waterslager but it's most likely origin was the Tyroler canary bred as a stroke bird with a nightingale accent. These birds were exported from Imst in Austria to a number of countries in Europe also ending up in Belgium, where a 6-inch Dutch canary was being bred. By crossing these two birds song canaries were bred, especially in the area of Mechelen in Belgium, with a characteristic nightingale accent. Theses are true stroke birds that differ clearly from the Harzer roller. The popularity of the Waterslager has spread to cover a large area of Europe where they are known as the ultimate nightingale singer.

The Timbrado

The Timbrado is relatively young breed of song canary that originated as the Spanish Timbrado, a descendent of the wild canary. It's thanks mainly to the efforts of Spanish breeders that it developed its own song, but it can't compare with the song of either the Harzer or the Waterslager. The Timbrado is somewhat smaller than the Harzer and, even though it can be any one of the known canary colours, it's commonly black with yellow (green). Even crested examples turn up from time to time. It's notable though that not only has the red factor not been bred into these birds, it's even considered to be an undesirable colour. The Timbrado nearly always sings with a half open beak, rarely with it closed. The

Timbrado

Waterslager

Timbrado

vowels and consonants in the alphabet can be heard in the Timbrado's song. An experienced songbird breeder who's able to recognise the hard and soft tones in the song hears the bird 'speak'.

Type canaries

Physical characteristics such as posture, size, shape, plumage, and in some cases patterns in the plumage, differentiate "type" canaries from the song and colour canaries and these individual characteristics have been developed still further to create varieties that display even more breed specific attributes.

Colour canaries

Due to the use of increasingly selective captive breeding methods, the original characteristics of the grey-green coloured canaries found in the Canary Islands, and the long plumage that provided protection against the substantial temperature differences found there, are gradually disappearing. Each change that came about in the colour in the process was retained and refined to produce birds with increasing amounts of yellow visible behind the darker colouring of their plumage.

These birds, known as colour canaries, are also often kept today for their song. Further selective breeding produced yellow canaries that lacked any dark colouring at all.

positive tours it sings are variable, delivered short and fast and, possibly because of its Spanish character, full of temperament. Twelve unique tours are recognised in total divided into continuous, lightly interrupted and interrupted. It's possibly not so obvious to less experienced fanciers but nearly all

Colour canaries are divided into three groups:

- variegated canaries, that have yellow as well as darker feather areas
- lipochrome canaries, with pure yellow plumage
- melanin canaries, with darker colour pigmentation in their plumage interwoven with yellow

Variegated canaries

Variegated canaries have irregularly coloured plumage with darker as well as yellow colouring. In one specimen the majority of the plumage may be dark, in another the darker colouring will be confined to just a few small patches or streaks. Their appearance and song make them good household pets.

Plumage colour

The emphasis with colour canaries is on the dispersal of colours in the plumage but apart from adding to their appearance colours also have a function. Amongst other uses, colour can serve as camouflage, an attribute found in ground breeding birds, but it can also help birds of the same variety to recognise each other. Although the colours of some birds have changed over time for natural reasons, in the case of colour canaries the changes were brought about by the efforts of breeders.

Canaries are divided into two main groups depending upon the colours present in their plumage. These are the melanistic birds and the lipochrome birds. Plumage

Type canary

Isabel red intensive

eyes. Non- iridescent colours also occur but the majority of canary colours are pigment colours.

Melanistic colours
All colour canaries that display dark pigmentation to any degree in their plumage belong to this group. These colours, called melanin's, may or may not be combined with carotenoide or lipochrome, known in the past as fat-soluble colours. The melanistic or pigmented group is divided into the following colour varieties:
• Black
• Brown
• Agate
• Isabel

These colours make up the colour canary's four basic colours. Characteristics in the canary can cause these basic colours to muta-te leading to the creation of new names. In addition, these colours are always present in combination with a lipochrome colour.

Lipochrome colours
Canaries belonging to this group lack any inherited dark colouring in their plumage. The colour of these birds is dictated by the presence of a lipochrome colour. The lipochrome group is divided into the colours:
• yellow
• red
• white (this is not actually a colour but a colourless feather, in which only the material of the feather itself is visible)

can be coloured in different ways depending upon the structure and the type of colour. Feathers may have the sort of structure that reflects light similar to the way light is reflected from a thin layer of oil floating on water. These colours are known as structural colours. Feathers may also contain pigments or so called pigment colours, which look less metallic than structural colours. Pigment colours though are not limited to a bird's feathers and are also found in their beaks, legs and even the

Mutations

In addition to melanin and lipo-chrome, the colours displayed by canaries are influenced by muta-tion. There are three mutations: Intensive, Buff (or non-intensive) and mosaic.

Intensive

The long plumage of the wild canary protected it against the high daytime and the low night temperatures experienced in the Canary Islands. Feathers are a good insulation against heat when they are slightly raised and against the cold when they are held snu-gly against the body. Selective breeding produced birds with clear colours that fetched a higher market price than the less clear birds, and this resulted in further refinements that produced what is now called the intensity factor.

Buff, or non-intensive

Buff, is a naturally occurring canary mutation. The somewhat long plumage creates a phenome-non whereby the lipochrome colour present does not extend across the entire area of each fea-ther leaving a colourless fringe. When the feathers are laid over each other like roof tiles, the frin-ges produce a colour softening effect or so-called buff separation.

Mosaic

Although the red factor appeared in canaries within a couple of years of the hybridisation of the

Red Siskin, another characteristic responsible for secondary sexual characteristics and markings appeared in the female, which cle-arly differentiated her from the male. This differentiation is called "sexual dimorphism" and is also present in the Red Siskin. Further selective breeding produced a female canary with markings that became known as mosaic markings, a characteristic that was also developed in males so that today two types of mosaic canaries are recognised.

A combination of melanistic colour mutations and lipochrome colour mutations can produce more than one a hundred different, definable canary colours.

Black with white recessive intensive

Black variety

Intensive birds have brilliant blue bodies and beautifully coloured black wing and tail feathers with small and sharply defined stripes on the back and thin striping on the flanks. The horny parts such as the beak, feet, toes and nails are tinted deep black. Brown hasn't developed in the feathers and the lipochrome colour is uniform over the entire body.

Buff birds in general have browner plumage, which produces a brownish back and can lead to a fringe developing on the flight feathers. Mosaic birds' underbodies and pants, which extend well above the thighbone, are white. Flight feather pigmentation is black. The colour of the back is the same as in non-mosaic birds and this has to be taken into account when considering possibilities that are achievable when matching a particular male to a particular female. The overall effect of colour variations in the black variety is strongly influenced by the lipochrome colour and mutation.

Most common colours
- black with yellow intensive
- black with red intensive
- black with yellow non-intensive
- black with red non-intensive
- black with yellow mosaic type 1 or 2
- black with red mosaic type 1 or 2
- black with yellow ivory intensive
- black with red ivory intensive
- black with yellow ivory non-intensive
- black with red ivory non-intensive
- black with yellow ivory mosaic type 1 or 2
- black with red ivory mosaic type 1 or 2
- black with white dominant intensive
- black with white recessive intensive
- black with white dominant non-intensive
- black with white recessive non-intensive

Brown variety

The influence of the intensive factor in intensive birds reduces the amount of brown visible between the striping. The striping itself is a dark brown colour also found in the wing and tail feathers. The horny parts are mid brown. Because of the reduction in the amount of brown between the striping and the influence of the intensive factor on the lipochrome colour, neither of the brown colours on the back is overlapping. The plumage of Buff birds usually has more brown in it, which results in a brownish back. The striping should spread as far as possible but it does not have to be the same brown that's visible between the striping. The degree of brown present creates a warm brown tint, but this may not be so dominant as to make the lipochrome barely visible or invisible. Buff females in general will dis-

Black grey wing red mosaic type 2

Black opal white recessive

play the warmest brown tints. The same demands are placed on pigmentation in mosaic birds as in non-mosaic birds. Consideration always needs to be given to the possibilities that are achievable when matching a particular male to a particular female.

In brown variety mosaics the lower body and the pants are white to well above the thighbone. The overall effect of colour variations in the brown variety is strongly influenced by presence of the lipochrome colour in combination with the mutation.

Most common colours
• brown with yellow intensive
• brown with red intensive
• brown with yellow non-intensive
• brown with red non-intensive
• brown with yellow mosaic
  type 1 or 2
• brown with red mosaic
  type 1 or 2
• brown with yellow ivory intensive
• brown with red ivory intensive
• brown with yellow ivory
  non-intensive
• brown with red ivory
  non-intensive
• brown with yellow ivory
  mosaic type 1 or 2
• brown with red ivory mosaic
  type 1 or 2
• brown with white dominant
• brown with recessive white

Agate variety
Agate variety intensive birds have relatively dark wing and tail fea-

thers. The small, short back striping is a dark to practically black colour. Due to reduction in brown and the effect of the intensive factor, hardly any brown remains visible on the back. The horny parts are light and one colour but they may not be too dark or as dark as birds of the black variety.

Buff birds have a slightly larger, more sharply defined striping with somewhat reduced brown showing between the striping. This is also often the case with the flight feather fringes. The beard pattern is clearly marked on both sides. A silver veil is visible on the back of mosaic mutations in the agate series. The lower body and belly are white. Mosaic birds exhibit a lighter colour tint than the non-mosaic birds with the amount of pigmentation present being determined by the action of the mosaic factor and the sex.

By a process of selection, breeders succeeded in producing agate mosaics in about 1994 that exhibited a clear white zone bordered by a rather broad deep black striping. Both the brown and the lipochrome colours had disappeared. The final result was a bird with a sharply defined mosaic pattern that was somewhat clearer than the 'normal' agate mosaic. The overall effect of colour variations in the agate variety is strongly influenced by the lipochrome colour and the mutation.

Brown opal yellow-mosaic type 1

Brown pastel red mosaic type 1

Brown red mosaic type 2

Brown red non-intensive

Agate opal yellow
intensive

Most common colours
- agate with yellow intensive
- agate with red intensive
- agate with yellow non-intensive
- agate with red non-intensive
- agate with yellow mosaic
  type 1 or 2
- agate with red mosaic type 1 or 2
- agate with yellow ivory intensive
- agate with red ivory intensive
- agate with yellow ivory
  non-intensive
- agate with red ivory non-intensive
- agate with yellow ivory mosaic
  type 1 or 2
- agate with red ivory mosaic
  type 1 or 2
- agate with white dominant
- agate with white recessive

Isabel variety
A light brown colour is all that remains in the intensive bird's back markings, flight and tail feathers, flanks and down. Due to the reduction in brown and the effect of the intensive factor, brown is barely visible between the striping. The depth of colour in the brown striping and the tint can be slightly strengthened by the presence of a vague blue pattern. Buff birds posses a little more brown than the intensive birds and brown is displayed between the stripes. In addition they have a finely spread striping which makes the back look as though it's hardly striped at all, displaying

Agate yellow
mosaic type 1

more of an overall light brown colour. The same light brown colour is found in the plumage of mosaic birds. The lower body and the pants are white. The actual colour displayed is dictated by the mosaic factor in combination with the sex. The overall effect of colour variations in the Isabel variety is strongly influenced by the presence of the lipochrome colour and the mutation.

Most common colours
- Isabel with yellow intensive
- Isabel with red intensive
- Isabel with yellow non-intensive
- Isabel with red non-intensive
- Isabel with yellow mosaic type 1 or 2
- Isabel with red mosaic type 1 or 2
- Isabel with yellow ivory intensive
- Isabel with red ivory intensive
- Isabel with yellow ivory non-intensive
- Isabel with red ivory non-intensive
- Isabel with yellow ivory mosaic type 1 or 2
- Isabel with red ivory mosaic type 1 or 2
- Isabel with white dominant
- Isabel with white recessive

Yellow variety
Intensive birds have a pure deep yellow colour that covers the entire plumage including the flight and tail feathers. The full effect of the intensive factor is necessary to obtain an intensive colour. Buff

Isabel pastel red ivory mosaic type 1

birds are a pure light yellow colour that must be as evenly tinted as possible. The normal balanced buff distribution gives the bird a beautifully soft colour. To ensure that the mosaic markings are sharp and clearly recognisable, maximum yellow needs to be present in combination with a normal buff distribution.

Most common colours
- yellow intensive
- yellow non-intensive
- yellow mosaic type 1 or 2
- yellow ivory intensive
- yellow ivory non-intensive
- yellow ivory mosaic type 1 or 2

Red variety
Intensive birds have a deep, pure

Isabel pastel yellow schimmel

Satinet yellow intensive

Agate eumo yellow

and evenly distributed red colour over their entire plumage and the wing and tail feathers are evenly saturated and fully intensive. The horny parts are a light single colour. Buff birds have a deep, pure and evenly distributed red colour with a normal balanced buff distribution over the whole body. Mosaic bird markings are sharp and clearly visible. Where the mosaic markings are absent on the feathers, the colour is a clear white without any sign of red showing through.

Most common colours
• red intensive
• red non-intensive
• red mosaic type 1 or 2
• red ivory intensive
• red ivory non-intensive
• red ivory mosaic type 1 or 2

White variety
Mr Schrockius of Augsburg in Germany wrote a description of a white canary in 1667. In 1712 the French writer Hervieux also added white to his list of canary colours. Talk of white canaries

disappeared from about 1900 until 1910 when the colour appeared again in Germany and for some time it was called the German White. It began to spread again throughout Europe from about 1924 but the name now used is dominant white. By allowing limited luteine conversion to take place, it's possible for carotenoide colour deposits to appear in the outermost flight feathers. This deposit may be present in only the smallest quantity. Carotenoide colour is sometimes visible on the shoulders and the tail but this is wrong. Because the colour has become white, it's no longer possible to tell if it's an intensive bird or a buff bird. Nevertheless, these mutations are as much present in the dominant white as in any other colour variety. Intensive birds have a short plumage and often a colour that is too strong as a deposit on the edges of the wings. Buff birds have a somewhat less strongly coloured deposit. The plumage is a little longer and the down, especially, is longer and thicker than that of an intensive bird.

The dominant white is at its best with a light buff distribution. Preventing luteine conversion will prevent the mosaic pattern from appearing in the plumage.

With the exception of the lipochrome bird, dominant white will also appear in all basic colours of the melanin birds. The white colour as a rule is interwoven with the colour of the down.

Recessive white variety

In 1908, a Miss Lee in Martinborough near Wellington in New Zealand discovered a white canary in her aviary, however incest occurring there made it impossible to tell which parents the bird had come from.

Mr Kiesel of London in England bred a white canary at about the same time. Both canaries were pure white without any sign of a yellow tint. During further breeding, breeders came to the conclusion that these white canaries were not the same colour as the German white canaries, so to differentiate between the two the former became known as English White. The name was later changed to Recessive White to reflect the inherited factor responsible.

Red

Agate opal white recessive

Satinet white recessive

Lutino mosaic type 1

Agate opal
white recessive

Lutino ivory

A recessive white Canary's body is a clear white which causes a problem for breeders because the feathers quickly become polluted and lose their clarity. Intensive and buff mutations occur in recessive whites also.

Intensive birds have shorter feathers and often less down, which results in the plumage not fitting the body closely.
Non-intensive birds have a somewhat longer plumage, however the plumage will become too long if non-intensive birds are bred with other non-intensive birds over an extended period.

The recessive white is at its best as a light non-intensive bird. Preventing the conversion of luteine will stop the mosaic pattern from appearing in the plumage. With the exception of the lipochrome bird recessive white also appears in all the basic colours of the melanin birds.
Many more colour canary variations are appearing in addition to the varieties described as a result of the influence of a number of inherited characteristics, but the basic rule remains that it must always be possible to trace a colour back to one of the accepted basic colours.

Canary tips

The main consideration when keeping canaries is their health, which means that it becomes your responsibility from the moment you buy them. The hobby will place demands on your time and sometimes require effort so it's important to think things through carefully before you buy. Here are a few simple tips about buying, keeping and caring for canaries.

- Buy preferably ringed birds so that you have a reliable indication of their ages.
- Don't keep more birds than the space available to you will comfortably accommodate. Over-populating will not be beneficial to your bird's health.
- Apart from clean fresh seed and supplements make sure that clean drinking water is available every day. A canary can't go a single day without water.
- Make sure clean bathwater is available and replace it when it becomes polluted.
- Make sure that the cage or aviary includes the right type of perches. If perch bars are too thin, the canary's nails will grow too long
- Nails that have become too long should be cut carefully to avoid

cutting into an artery.
- Good hygiene and regular cleaning of the cage or aviary should prevent sicknesses from developing.
- Never expose a canary that's kept in the living room to more than 15 hours of daylight per day.
- If your bird isn't sick don't give it any medicine. If you do need to give it medicine follow the instructions concerning dosage strictly. Don't forget to take the size of the bird into consideration relative to the medicine being given.
- Don't let you canaries bred more than twice per year. The breeding season is exhausting for the birds.
- Don't unnecessarily disturb breeding birds during the breeding season. It's OK to check the nest but it needs to be done with care.

Internet Canaries

www.thesca.org.uk/guides/canaries/index.html
The Society for conservation in aviculture provides on this website information regarding breeding, feeding, housing and more.

www.geocities.com/ycc_uk/home page.html
The Yorkshire Canary club.

www.geocities.com/brian_keenan_uk
A breeders website with lot's of information on housing, management, breeding, moulting, articles and much more.

www.netcomuk.co.uk/~ncabirds/VETS.htm
A list of avian veterinarians in England.

www.netcomuk.co.uk/~ncabirds/NCA.htm
National Council For Aviculture (N.C.A.) U.K.

www.robirda.com
A place for Canaries, your source for small pet bird resources. Here you can learn how to keep your pet canary or finch happy, healthy, and full of song.

www.birdhotline.com
The goal is to reunite lost birds with their families, and with their heartwarming Bird Stories increase the public's awareness of the wonder of birds-these loving, warm, caring, intelligent little beings with wings, and to improve the quality of their lives.

Other books from About Pets

- The Border Collie
- The Boxer
- The Cavalier King Charles Spaniel
- The Cocker Spaniel
- The Dalmatian
- The Dobermann
- The German Shepherd
- The Golden Retriever
- The Jack Russell Terrier
- The Labrador Retriever
- The Puppy
- The Rottweiler
- The Budgerigar
- The Cockatiel
- The Lovebird
- The Parrot
- The Cat
- The Kitten
- The Dwarf Hamster
- The Dwarf Rabbit
- The Ferret
- The Gerbil
- The Guinea Pig
- The Hamster
- The Mouse
- The Rabbit
- The Rat
- The Goldfish
- The Tropical Fish
- The Snake

Key features of the series are:
- Most affordable books
- Packed with hands-on information
- Well written by experts
- Easy to understand language
- Full colour original photography
- 70 to 110 photos
- All one needs to know to care well for their pet
- Trusted authors, veterinary consultants, breed and species expert authorities
- Appropriate for first time pet owners
- Interesting detailed information for pet professionals
- Title range includes books for advanced pet owners and breeders
- Includes useful addresses, veterinary data, breed standards.

Black opalyellow
mozaik type 1

The Canary

Latin name:	*Serinus canarius*
English name:	Canary
Origin:	Canary Islands
Habitat:	Woods, gardens and parks
Length:	11 - 12 cm (4.3 – 4.75 in.)
Number of eggs:	3 - 5
Brooding time:	13 - 14 days
Life expectancy:	8 - 14 years (up to maximum 30 years)
Biorhythm:	Active by day